Contents

Alphabetically by Song Title

Patsy Cline

1973

Foremost female exponent of the Nashville Sound, Patsy Cline

The parents of Virginia Patterson Hensley named their daughter for the state where she was born in 1932. Marriage changed her name in 1953. Early in 1957, Patsy's performance of "Walking After Midnight" on an episode of *Arthur Godfrey's Talent Scouts* led to her hit recording of the tune. Its acceptance by country and pop buyers foretold even more spectacular achievements as a pioneering crossover artist, the first of a new breed of female country vocalists.

Patsy Cline moved to Nashville in 1960 and joined the Grand Ole Opry cast. She arrived just as the Nashville Sound was taking form, and her voice adapted perfectly to the new style. Coached by Decca producer Owen Bradley, she became one of the Nashville Sound's most expert interpreters, as her renditions of these three tunes reveal. Each is a yearning love ballad, a type of song she brought to life as few artists could. Cline's version of "Crazy" a song penned by Willie Nelson, peaked at No. 2 in *Billboard's* country charts and made it to No. 9 in the magazine's pop rankings. Although her recordings of "I Fall to Pieces" and "She's Got You" were slightly less impressive in pop chart performance, both were No. 1 country hits. All three songs have been recorded by numerous pop and country singers since Patsy first sang them early in the 1960s.

A plane crash on March 5, 1963, cut short Patsy Cline's life, yet her recordings had already secured her place in music history. Cline was elected to the Hall of Fame in 1973.

Smooth country crooner Patsy Cline, with her producer Paul Cohen at right

Patsy Cline at home

Crazy

Words and Music by
WILLIE NELSON

I Fall to Pieces

Words and Music by HANK COCHRAN
and HARLAN HOWARD

Moderate Country 2

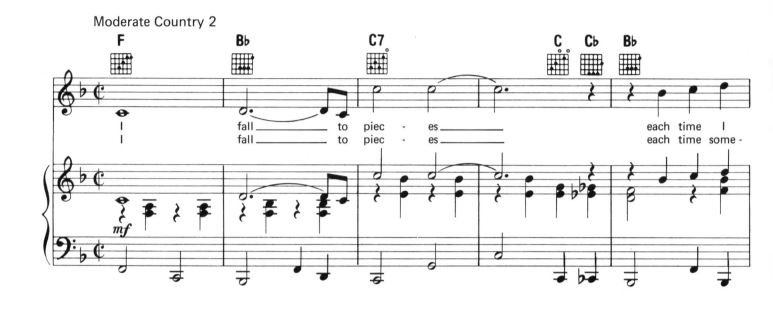

I
I fall _____ to piec - es _____ each time I
fall _____ to piec - es _____ each time some-

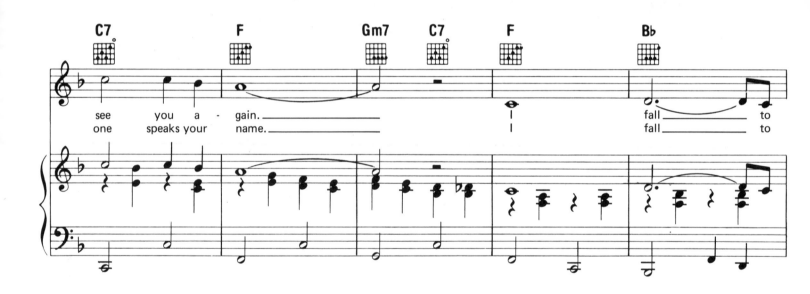

see you a - gain. _____ I fall _____ to
one speaks your name. _____ I fall _____ to

piec - es, _____ How can I be just your friend?
piec - es, _____ Time on - ly adds to the flame.

She's Got You

Words and Music by
HANK COCHRAN

Jim Denny

1966

Promoter and publisher Jim Denny

James Rae Denny, a prominent figure in country music's past, was born in Tennessee in 1911. As a youth, he found employment as a shipping clerk for the National Life and Accident Insurance Company, parent organization to radio station WSM. Working his way up in the Nashville-based firm, Denny began to take an interest in the Grand Ole Opry. By 1946 he was running the WSM Artists Bureau, which booked the station's country and pop entertainers. Before long, he was managing the Opry itself.

In 1953 Denny and Opry powerhouse Webb Pierce organized the Cedarwood Publishing Company. Following a dispute with WSM management about this enterprise, Denny left the station in 1956 to start his own talent agency. Denny's publishing, booking, and promotion activities accelerated the growth of Nashville's music industry. He died in 1963, still in his prime. Election to the Hall of Fame came three years later, in 1966.

"The Long Black Veil" and "Ruby, Don't Take Your Love to Town" are two treasures from the Cedarwood storehouse. Songwriters Danny Dill and Marijohn Wilkin deliberately penned "The Long Black Veil" in a folk vein and, with help from Lefty Frizzell's 1959 top-ten recording of the tune, added a gem to country music's rich lode of story songs. Just as powerful a tale is "Ruby, Don't Take Your Love to Town," a number that sprang from the fertile imagination of country writer-performer Mel Tillis. Kenny Rogers achieved a crossover hit with this song in 1969.

Grand Ole Opry manager, music publisher, and promoter Jim Denny, flanked by son Bill (left) and publisher Charlie Lamb

Bill Denny (left) with his famous father Jim

The Long Black Veil

Words and Music by MARIJOHN WILKIN
and DANNY DILL

Ruby, Don't Take Your Love to Town

Words and Music by
MEL TILLIS

Red Foley

1967

Red Foley

Clyde Julian Foley (1910–1968) spent his boyhood in Kentucky before moving to Chicago as a young man. One of several southern musicians recruited by John Lair for Chicago's WLS *National Barn Dance*, Red Foley played guitar and sang with Lair in the popular Cumberland Ridge Runners band. Later Foley helped Lair organize the *Renfro Valley Barn Dance*, a radio show broadcast over stations in Cincinnati and Louisville. Returning to WLS in the early 1940s, Foley ascended rapidly as a solo performer.

In 1946 the smooth-singing, pop-influenced baritone replaced leather-lunged Roy Acuff as Grand Ole Opry headliner. This change symbolized the stylistic changes then affecting country music. During his seven-year stay on the Opry, Foley recorded several trendy "boogie" songs, including "Chattanoogie Shoe Shine Boy." This recording shot to the summit of both country *and* pop charts in 1950, a feat seldom equalled before or since. Like country music in general, however, Foley's material included gospel numbers such as "Peace in the Valley." Foley's rendition of this song became a No. 7 country hit in 1951. "Old Shep," a touching story of a boy and his dog, was also a popular Foley tune of the same period, revealing his sure handling of sentimental topics.

For most of the 1950s, Foley hosted *Jubilee USA*, a nationally televised program originating from Springfield, Missouri. He returned to Nashville in the mid-1960s and won election to the Hall of Fame in 1967, one year before his death.

.

One of country music's most popular performers, whether on radio, TV, film or records – Red Foley

Clyde Julian "Red" Foley, popular and versatile star of the *National Barn Dance*, Grand Ole Opry, & *Ozark Jubilee*

Chattanoogie Shoe Shine Boy

Words and Music by HARRY STONE
and JACK STAPP

24

Old Shep

Words and Music by
CLYDE "RED" FOLEY

(There'll Be)
Peace in the Valley
(For Me)

Words and Music by
THOMAS A. DORSEY

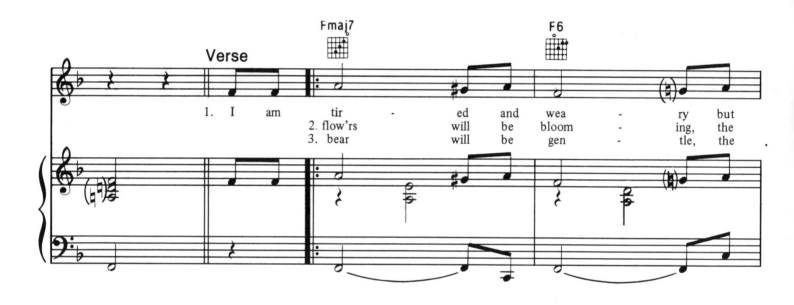

1. I am tir - ed and wea - ry but
2. flow'rs will be bloom - ing, the
3. bear will be gen - tle, the

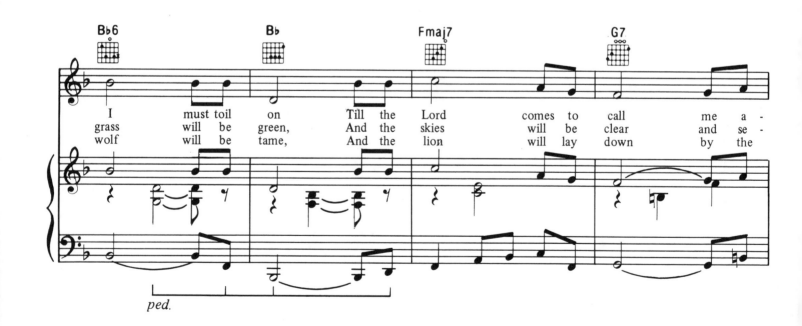

I must toil on Till the Lord comes to call me a -
grass will be green, And the skies will be clear
wolf will be tame, And the lion will lay down by the

ped.

Verse 4

4. No head-aches or heart-aches or misunderstands
   No confusion or trouble won't be
   No frowns to defile just a big endless smile,
   There'll be peace and contentment for me.

Connie B. Gay

1980

Country promoter and TV pioneer
Connie B. Gay

Connie B. Gay (1914–1989), born in Lizard Lick, North Carolina, was one of country music's foremost businessmen. After graduating from the University of North Carolina in Raleigh, he served as soil analyst, administrator, speech writer, and radio producer for the United States Department of Agriculture, working not only in North Carolina, but also in Washington, D.C., and the Virgin Islands.

Thoroughly familiar with rural listeners, Gay perceptively appreciated country music's growing urban audience as well. Assembling a radio and television empire headquartered in Arlington, Virginia, he produced hundreds of country shows during the twenty-five years following World War II. *Town and Country Time*, one of his most widely syndicated programs, began in 1954 and starred Jimmy Dean. "Ridin' Down to Santa Fe" was the theme song for this series.

As his broadcasting realm expanded, Gay became the East Coast's top country music concert promoter. In both capacities, he advanced performers' careers at all levels of the industry. Grand Ole Opry veteran Billy Grammer was one artist who got his start in the Washington, D.C., area with help from Connie B. Gay. "Gotta Travel On," a 1959 country hit, is Grammer's trademark number.

An organizer of the Country Music Association and the Country Music Foundation, Gay was elected to the Hall of Fame in 1980.

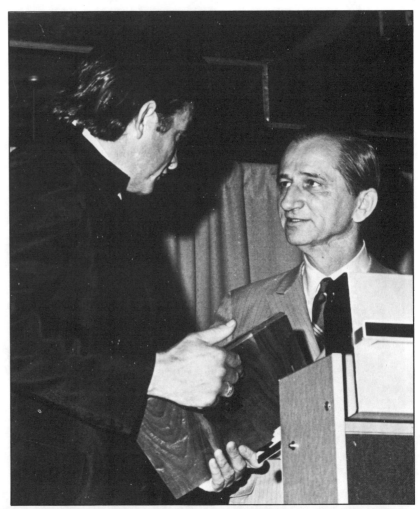

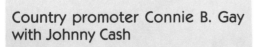

Country promoter Connie B. Gay with Johnny Cash

Flanked by Barbara Mandrell and Mac Davis, Connie B. Gay receives his Hall of Fame plaque, 1980

Ridin' Down to Santa Fe

Words and Music by
JOHNNY BOND

Rid - in' down_____ to San - ta Fe,_____
Rid - in' down_____ to San - ta Fe,_____

Just be - yond the moun - tains and a - cross the way;
Gon - na see the boss and I'll col - lect my pay;

See that sun hang low in the west,_____
Need a hun - dred dol - lars or more,

Gotta Travel On

Words and Music by PAUL CLAYTON, LARRY EHRLICH,
DAVID LAZAR and TOM SIX

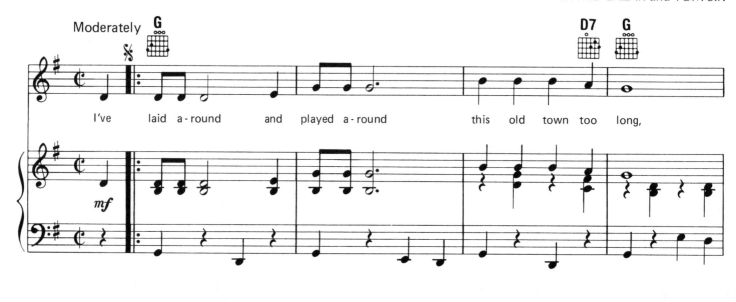

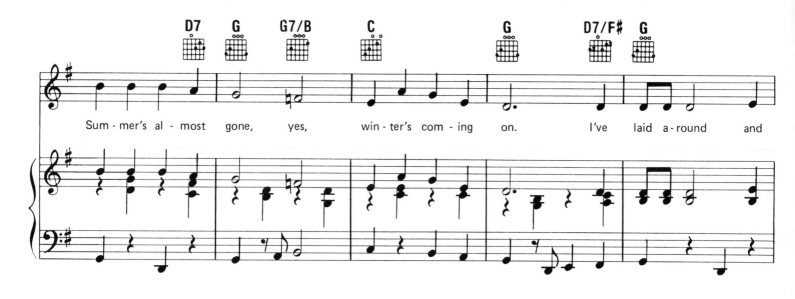

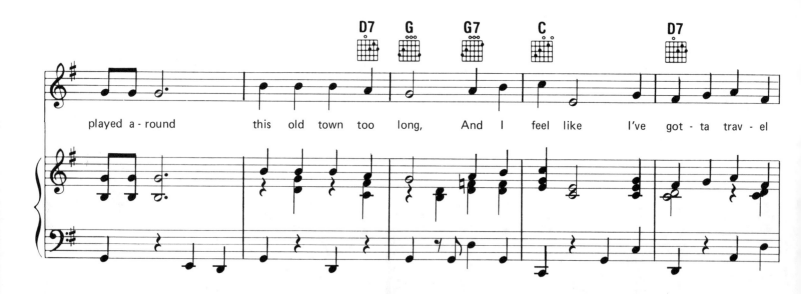

Grandpa Jones

1978

Louis Marshall "Grandpa" Jones

Louis Marshall Jones (1913–1998) was from rural Kentucky. Already a proficient musician in his youth, Jones began to adopt the persona of an old-timer, at first to match a voice that sounded older than his years. During the 1930s and early 1940s, Jones toured the Northeast and performed on WWVA in Wheeling, West Virginia, and WLW in Cincinnati. After military service in Germany, where he entertained American troops over the Armed Forces Radio Network, he came to the Grand Ole Opry in 1946.

Tradition-minded audiences loved Jones' high-kicking, foot-stomping rendition of "Eight More Miles to Louisville," best-seller on the King label during the late 1940s. "Old Rattler's Pup" is one of several follow-up tunes to "Old Rattler," another early Jones hit. The novelty song "Mountain Dew," by Bascom Lamar Lunsford and Scotty Wiseman, is so strongly identified with Jones that many fans think he wrote it. Jones' exuberant showmanship, old-timey banjo style, and colorful humor helped to uphold traditional forms through over fifty years of modernization in country music. For decades he often performed with his wife Ramona, an excellent singer and fiddler; their husband-and-wife act also preserved a country music tradition.

Once a regular on *Hee-Haw*, Grandpa Jones received his Hall of Fame award in 1978.

One of country music's funniest performers, long-time Grand Ole Opry favorite Grandpa Jones.

"Everybody's Grandpa"
— Grandpa Jones

Eight More Miles to Louisville

Words and Music by
LOUIS MARSHALL JONES

Lively, but not too fast

I've

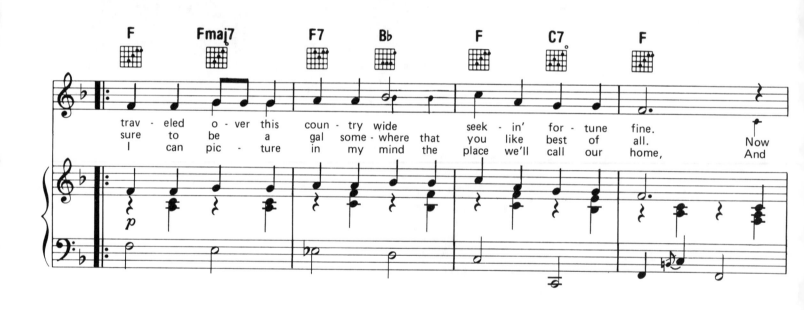

trav - eled o - ver this coun - try wide seek - in' for - tune fine. Now
sure to be a gal some - where that you like best of all. And

Up and down the two coast lines I've trav - eled ev' - ry - where, From
mine is down in Lou - is - ville, she's long and she is tall, But
from those lit - tle tots for two we'll nev - er want to roam. The

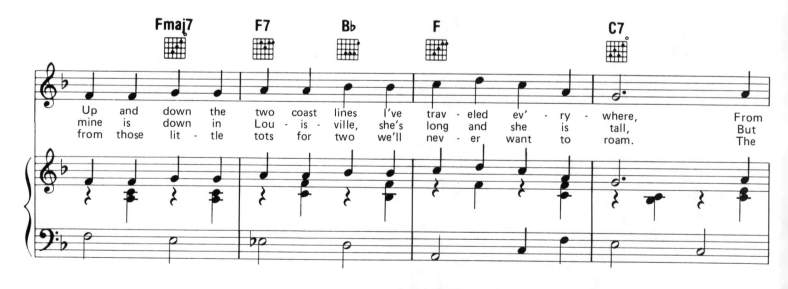

Mountain Dew

Words and Music by SCOTT WISEMAN
and BASCOMB LUNSFORD

Old Rattler's Pup

Traditional

Moderately Bright

1. The woods will ring a - gain to - night with a voice I love to hear.

Up from the val - ley, it's a - roll - in' loud and clear. 2. With my

old shot gun and far back light be - neath a yel - low moon, I'm out to - night to

see a fight of a big ring deer ra - coon. Old Rat - tler

left us years a - go, but Rat - tler's pup is a - com - in' up, you ought to see him

go. go.

D.C. for additional verses

Additional Verses:

3. At fifteen after eleven o'clock
   He got a red hot trail
   And from the noise you'd think he had
   That old coon by the tail.

4. Well, he run him up a white oak tree
   Way out on a limb
   And there by the light by the yellow moon
   I got a glimpse of him. (CHORUS)

5. When that old coon looked down at me
   He was a sight to see
   He looked as big as a grizzly bear
   Perched up in that tree.

6. I cut the tree, down come the coon
   And when he hit the ground
   Rattler's Pup and old man coon
   Went around and 'round and 'round.

7. They fought all night and all day long
   It was a fearful sight
   No better coon, no better dog
   Got ever in a fight. (CHORUS)

Loretta Lynn

1988

The young Loretta Lynn fresh from Butcher Holler, Kentucky

As even the most casual country fan will likely know, Loretta Webb Lynn was born a coal miner's daughter. The year was 1935 and the place was Butcher Holler, Kentucky, also the locale of her marriage at age thirteen to Oliver Doolittle "Mooney" Lynn. Encouraged by Mooney, Loretta started singing professionally while in her twenties, and in 1960 she scored her first minor hit with a song she wrote, "Honky Tonk Girl." The Lynns moved to Nashville shortly thereafter, and in 1962 Loretta joined the Grand Ole Opry. By 1972, the year the CMA voted her Entertainer of the Year, her straight-ahead country vocals, feisty songs, and down-home personal charm had made her one of the most popular stars in the history of country music.

Rarely has one song done as much for an artist as "Coal Miner's Daughter" did for Loretta Lynn. Written by her, it gave her a No. 1 record in 1970, a title for her best-selling autobiography, and a title for the hit 1980 movie based on that book. In the movie, one of the more amusing scenes revolves around Loretta (Sissy Spacek) writing "You Ain't Woman Enough" in response to catching Mooney (Tommy Lee Jones) fooling around with another woman. Though not a Lynn original, "Blue Kentucky Girl" sounded like it could have been. It proved one of her most memorable records and was revived many years later by Emmylou Harris.

Loretta Lynn was elected to the Hall of Fame in 1988.

Loretta Lynn at the Grand Ole Opry

The life of Loretta Lynn was the subject of the major motion picture *Coal Miner's Daughter* (1980)

Blue Kentucky Girl

Words and Music by
JOHNNY MULLINS

He left me for the bright lights of the town.
Don't wait to bring great rich - es home to me.

A coun - try boy ___ set
I need no dia - mond

Coal Miner's Daughter

Words and Music by
LORETTA LYNN

You Ain't Woman Enough

Words and Music by
LORETTA LYNN

Marty Robbins

1982

Informal pose of the popular and multi-talented Marty Robbins

Martin David Robinson (1925–1982) was one of nine children born to a poor Arizona family. He turned from odd jobs to professional musicianship in the mid-1940s, and by 1953 he was recording for Columbia and singing full-time on the Grand Old Opry. A singer-songwriter unequalled in versatility, the effervescent performer easily applied his rich voice to calypso, pop, cowboy, Hawaiian and mainstream country material. His records appeared in the country singles charts during every year between 1953 and 1982.

The second of Robbins' many No. 1 hits, "Singing the Blues," was written by Arkansan Melvin Endsley, who pitched the song to Robbins personally at a Grand Ole Opry show. Topping the country charts in 1956, Robbins' disc also rose to No. 28 in the pop charts. Robbins recorded "A White Sport Coat" in 1957 at a New York session, backed by Ray Conniff's orchestra and Mitch Miller's chorus. A massive country and pop hit, this tale of lost love confirmed Robbins' nickname "Mr. Teardrop." Robbins expressed his love of the Old West in the story song "El Paso," recorded in 1959 for the album *Gunfighter Ballads and Trail Songs*. Later released as a single, "El Paso" became a million-seller and won the entertainer a 1961 Grammy for Best Country and Western Performance.

Marty Robbins died in December 1982, just two months after accepting Hall of Fame honors.

A master of many styles who was consistently popular from the early 1950s until his death in 1982, Marty Robbins

The effervescent Marty Robbins

El Paso

Words and Music by
MARTY ROBBINS

Moderato

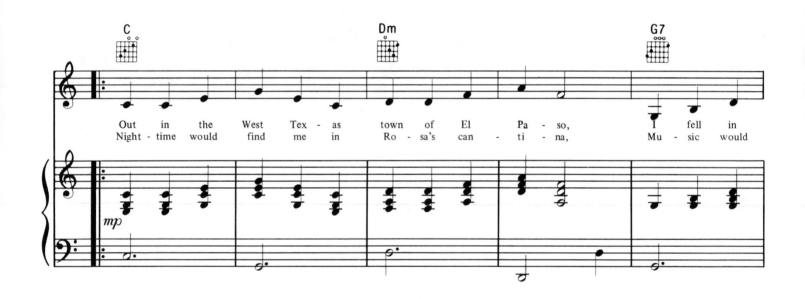

Out in the West Tex - as town of El Pa - so,   I fell in
Night - time would find me in Ro - sa's can - ti - na,   Mu - sic would

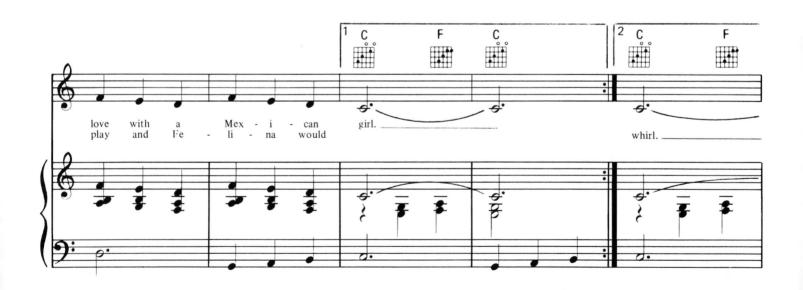

love with a Mex - i - can girl. _____
play and Fe - li - na would   whirl. _____

CODA (after last verse)

D.S. al Coda

Singing the Blues

Words and Music by
MELVIN ENDSLEY

A White Sport Coat
(And a Pink Carnation)

Words and Music by
MARTY ROBBINS

Fred Rose

1961

Songwriter, music publisher, record producer, and well-respected gentleman: Fred Rose

Knols Fred Rose, one of country music's greatest songwriters, was born in Indiana in 1898 and spent much of his life as a Tin Pan Alley musician. Between 1933 and 1942, Rose worked in Nashville and Hollywood, writing hits for Gene Autry and other entertainers, pop and country alike. In 1942 Rose and Grand Old Opry headliner Roy Acuff created Acuff-Rose Publications, Nashville's first major music publishing house.

A superb talent scout, producer, and promoter, Rose nurtured the careers of many artists and songwriters, Hank Williams chief among them. Rose died in 1954, but not before he had seen Nashville's emergence as Music City. His 1961 election to the Hall of Fame as a charter member underscored the importance of his many contributions to country music.

These three selections capture the range of Fred Rose's musical gifts. During the 1920s, when he lived in Chicago, " 'Deed I Do" was one of his biggest songwriting hits, recorded by a horde of pop vocalists. "Blues in My Mind" was tailored for the hot western swing band of Paul Howard, an Opry star of the mid-1940s. In 1945 Rose himself cut this tune for Columbia as The Rambling Rogue. "Blue Eyes Crying in the Rain," recorded by Roy Acuff, Elton Britt, and other country singers in the late 1940s, is the song that launched Willie Nelson to superstardom as a recording artist in 1975. Nelson's first No. 1 country hit also climbed high in pop trade-paper charts.

A young
Fred Rose
at the piano.

Fred Rose — master songsmith, song
publisher, and record producer.

Blue Eyes Crying in the Rain

Words and Music by
FRED ROSE

Blues in My Mind

Words and Music by
FRED ROSE

Blues in 2

C

I   ought to   hate you   for these   blues   in my
I'm   go - ing   hate cra - zy   with these   blues   in my

C7

C

mind.   What   makes me   love you?   Am I
mind.   How   can you   just keep   on con -

C7   **C**   **G**

los - ing my   mind?   I   won - der
fus - ing my   mind?   You've   got a

'Deed I Do

Words and Music by WALTER HIRSCH
and FRED ROSE

Arthur Satherley

1971

Lifelong champion of country music, the dapper Uncle Art Satherley

Englishman Arthur Edward Satherley (1889–1986) boarded a steamship for America at the age of twenty-three. At first he worked for the Wisconsin Chair Company, then manufacturing cabinets for phonograph makers. After 1917 Satherley became a jack-of-all-trades for Wisconsin Chair's Paramount label, supervising sessions, helping with record manufacturing, and promoting sales. From Paramount he moved to the American Record Corporation where he took on similar duties. The executive recorded both blues and country artists for Columbia Records between 1938 and 1952. From his Hollywood office, Satherley traveled thousands of miles annually on Columbia's behalf. Working with Roy Acuff, Gene Autry, Bob Wills, and a host of others, he held sessions in hotels, warehouses, professional studios, and even mountain cabins. "Uncle Art" saw record-making change from a primitive art into a modern science. A champion of country music long before it became fashionable, he won election to the Hall of Fame in 1971.

"Born to Lose" and "No Letter Today" were both hits for one of Satherley's hottest artists of the early 1940s — Texas-reared Ted Daffan. As tunesmith and recording star, Daffan created a classic weeper in "Born to Lose." His "No Letter Today" was well-timed for the emotional climate of World War II, which found many Americans anxiously awaiting word from a sweetheart at home or in military service. Al Dexter's performance of "Pistol Packin' Mama," a hit in both country and pop markets, was also covered successfully by Bing Crosby and the Andrews Sisters. All three of these honky-tonk anthems enjoyed lengthy jukebox lives during the war.

Uncle Art Satherley in his natural habitat, the recording studio

On the right, pioneer country A&R man Arthur Edward "Uncle Art" Satherley

Born to Lose

Words and Music by
TED DAFFAN

Born to lose, I've lived my life in vain;_____ Ev - 'ry
lose, my ev - 'ry hope is gone;_____ It's so

dream has on - ly brought me pain;_____ All my life I've
hard to face that emp - ty dawn;_____ You were all the

al - ways been so blue;_____ Born to lose and now I'm los - in'
hap - pi - ness I knew;_____ Born to lose and now I'm los - in'

91

No Letter Today

Words and Music by
TED DAFFAN

Pistol Packin' Mama

Words and Music by
AL DEXTER

Moderate Blues Tempo

1. Drink - in' beer in a cab - a - ret,__ And was I hav - in' fun! Un - til one night she
2. She kicked out my__ wind - shield, She hit me o - ver the head, She cussed and cried and
3. Drink - in' beer in a cab - a - ret,__ And dan - cing with a blonde, Un - til one night she

caught me right,__ And now I'm on the run.
said I'd lied,__ And wished that I was dead.   Lay that pis - tol down, Babe, Lay that pis - tol
shot out the light,__ Bang! that blonde was gone.

down,   Pis - tol Pack - in' Ma - ma,   Lay that pis - tol down!   down!

Hank Thompson

1989

Over the years, few artists have been able to match Hank Thompson's record as an exemplar of both the western swing and honky-tonk traditions in country music. Born in Waco, Texas, in 1925, Henry William "Hank" Thompson was starring on his own local radio show by the time he was sixteen. After a World War II stint in the navy, he returned to civilian life as a rising star of Texas country music. After a couple of small label releases did well for Thompson regionally, he was signed by Capitol Records in 1947. He scored his first chart hit one year later and continued charting into the 1980s. Throughout Thompson's peak years of activity, his band's smooth fusion of swing and honky-tonk styles made them a favorite in country dance halls and on jukeboxes across America.

Thompson's first major hit, reaching No. 2 in 1948 and spending thirty-eight weeks on the *Billboard* charts, was his own light-hearted "Humpty Dumpty Heart." It remained the biggest hit of his career until 1952, when he scored a No. 1 smash with his career record, the honky-tonk classic "The Wild Side of Life." Based on a durable melody shared with the Carter Family's "I'm Thinking Tonight of My Blue Eyes" and Roy Acuff's "The Great Speckled Bird," "The Wild Side of Life" would spend thirteen weeks at No. 1 in 1952. Ironically, the song that would knock it from the top of two of *Billboard's* charts would be Kitty Wells' "It Wasn't God Who Made Honky Tonk Angels," an answer song to Thompson's hit.

Hank Thompson was elected to the Hall of Fame in 1989.

Hank Thompson and Merle Travis

Hank Thompson with band, 1950s

Humpty Dumpty Heart

Words and Music by
HANK THOMPSON

The Wild Side of Life

Words and Music by WILLIAM WARREN
and ARLIE A. CARTER

Jo Walker-Meador

1995

Jo Walker-Meador at desk, 1958

As longtime executive director of the Country Music Association, Jo Walker-Meador was instrumental in raising country music's profile to its current level of popularity. Her tenure with the CMA saw the number of country radio stations grow from less than a hundred to over two thousand. Born in Orlinda, Tennessee, Walker-Meador joined the CMA as office manager in 1958, the year the organization was formed to help better promote country music in the marketplace. A tireless advocate for the industry, she was appointed executive director of the CMA in 1963 and held that position until 1991. Under her leadership, the CMA implemented many of its most important programs, including the creation and telecasting of the annual CMA awards and the creation of Fan Fair.

In 1967, the first year the CMA awards were held, the song voted Song of the Year was Dallas Frazier's "There Goes My Everything." Inspired by "a broken marriage between two friends of mine," Frazier once said, the song was a No. 1 smash for singer Jack Greene. Elvis Presley and Engelbert Humperdinck also had hits with Frazier's classic. In 1968, the CMA selected Bobby Russell's "Honey" as the Song of the Year. As sung by Bobby Goldsboro, "Honey" topped both the pop and country charts for several weeks in 1968.

Jo Walker-Meador was elected to the Hall of Fame in 1995.

Jo Walker-Meador with Buck Owens

There Goes My Everything

Words and Music by
DALLAS FRAZIER

Honey

Words and Music by
BOBBY RUSSELL

Kitty Wells

1976

Muriel Deason Wright, better known as Kitty Wells

Born in Nashville in 1919, Muriel Deason began performing at sixteen on that city's WSIX, where she met country singer Johnnie Wright. In 1937 she married Wright and in a few years he gave her the stage name Kitty Wells, taken from an old song by that title. During the 1940s, Kitty sang throughout the South with her husband and his partner Jack Anglin. The three musicians were on hand for the premiere of the *Louisiana Hayride*, aired over Shreveport's KWKH in April 1948. The Grand Old Opry beckoned when Johnnie & Jack started hitting on RCA Victor early in the 1950s, and Kitty went with the duo to WSM.

"It Wasn't God Who Made Honky Tonk Angels," recorded at Kitty's first Decca session, topped the country charts in 1952 and made her a star in her own right. She became the first female country artist of the postwar era to chart consistently. "Making Believe" was one of Kitty's most popular songs in 1955. Like "Heartbreak U.S.A.," a No. 1 country tune of 1961, it frankly expresses love's anguish from a woman's point of view. Kitty's unmistakably country voice has a hard edge and a "cry," tailor-made for the honky-tonk style that made her famous.

Kitty Wells won election to the Hall of Fame in 1976.

Kitty Wells, during the early years of her reign as "The Queen of Country Music"

The Queen of Country Music, Kitty Wells (third from left), surrounded by her "court," the Johnnie Wright-Kitty Wells Family Show

Heartbreak U.S.A.

Words and Music by
HARLAN HOWARD

It Wasn't God Who Made Honky Tonk Angels

Moderately

Words and Music by
J.D. MILLER

Making Believe

Words and Music by
JIMMY WORK

you'll nev-er be mine ___ mak-ing be-

lieve, ___ I'll spend my life-time ___

___ lov-ing you ___ mak-ing be-

lieve. ___ Mak-ing be-lieve. ___